ALIEN GRAVEYARD

by **Leah Kaminski**

Illustrations by Candy Briones

BEARPORT
PUBLISHING

Minneapolis, Minnesota

Credits

22T, © ElvisFontenot/iStock/Getty Images Plus; and 22B, © Taras Young/Wikimedia.

DISCLAIMER: This graphic story is a dramatization based on true events. It is intended to give the reader a sense of the narrative rather than a presentation of actual details as they occurred.

Library of Congress Cataloging-in-Publication Data

Names: Kaminski, Leah, author. | Briones, Candy, 1987– illustrator.
Title: Alien graveyard / by Leah Kaminski ; illustrations by Candy Briones.
Description: Bear claw. | Minneapolis, Minnesota : Bearport Publishing, [2020] | Series: Haunted history | Includes bibliographical references and index.
Identifiers: LCCN 2020008727 (print) | LCCN 2020008728 (ebook) | ISBN 9781647470098 (library binding) | ISBN 9781647470166 (paperback) | ISBN 9781647470234 (ebook)
Subjects: LCSH: Unidentified flying objects–Sightings and encounters–Juvenile literature. | Unidentified flying objects–Sightings and encounters–Comic books, strips, etc. | Graphic novels. | Graphic novels.
Classification: LCC TL789.2 .K36 2020 (print) | LCC TL789.2 (ebook) | DDC 001.942–dc23
LC record available at https://lccn.loc.gov/2020008727
LC ebook record available at https://lccn.loc.gov/2020008728

For more information, write to Bearport Publishing, 5357 Penn Avenue South, Minneapolis, MN 55419. Printed in the United States of America.

CONTENTS

ALIEN ENCOUNTERS

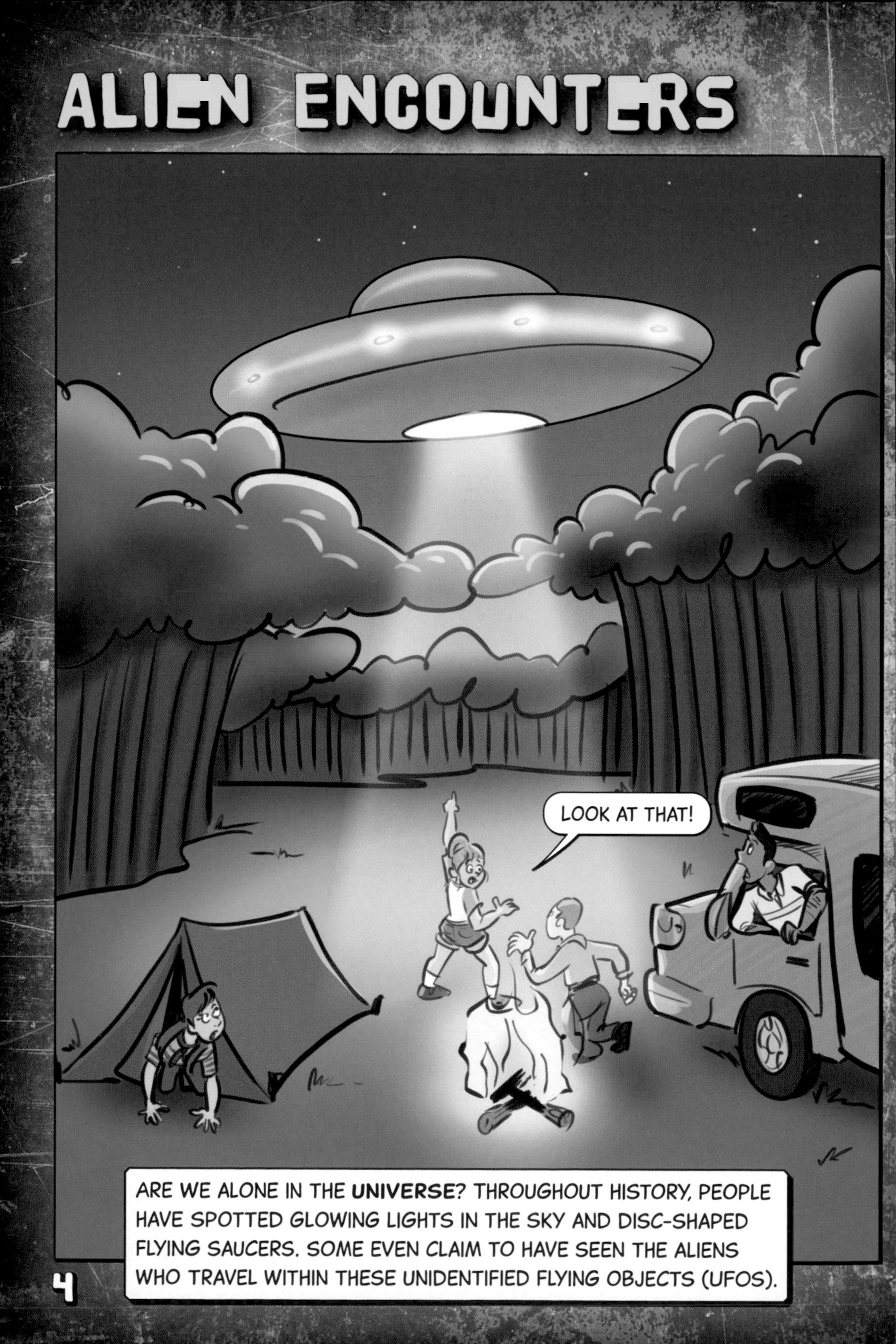
LOOK AT THAT!
ARE WE ALONE IN THE **UNIVERSE**? THROUGHOUT HISTORY, PEOPLE HAVE SPOTTED GLOWING LIGHTS IN THE SKY AND DISC-SHAPED FLYING SAUCERS. SOME EVEN CLAIM TO HAVE SEEN THE ALIENS WHO TRAVEL WITHIN THESE UNIDENTIFIED FLYING OBJECTS (UFOS).

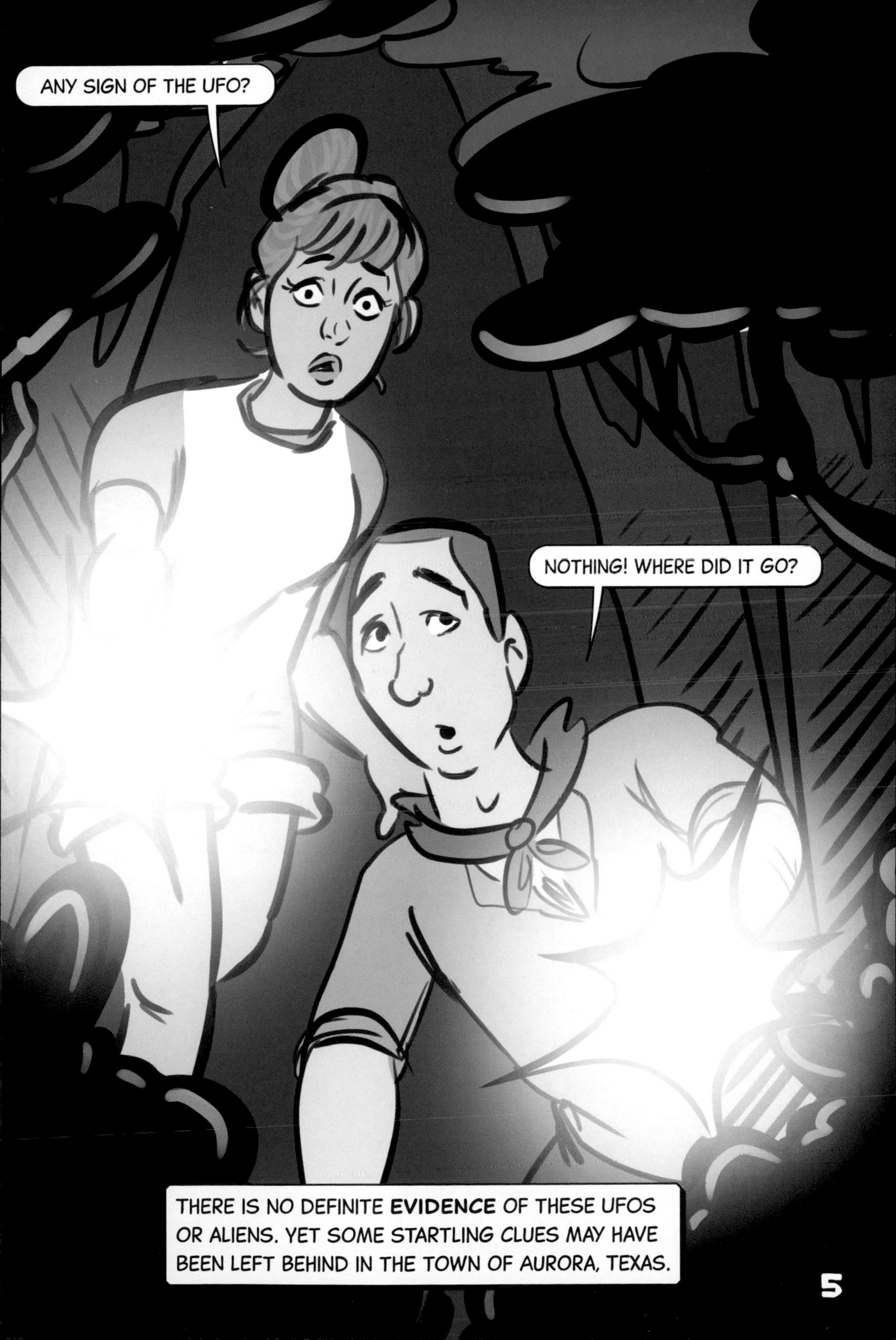
ANY SIGN OF THE UFO?
NOTHING! WHERE DID IT GO?
THERE IS NO DEFINITE **EVIDENCE** OF THESE UFOS OR ALIENS. YET SOME STARTLING CLUES MAY HAVE BEEN LEFT BEHIND IN THE TOWN OF AURORA, TEXAS.

THE CRASH

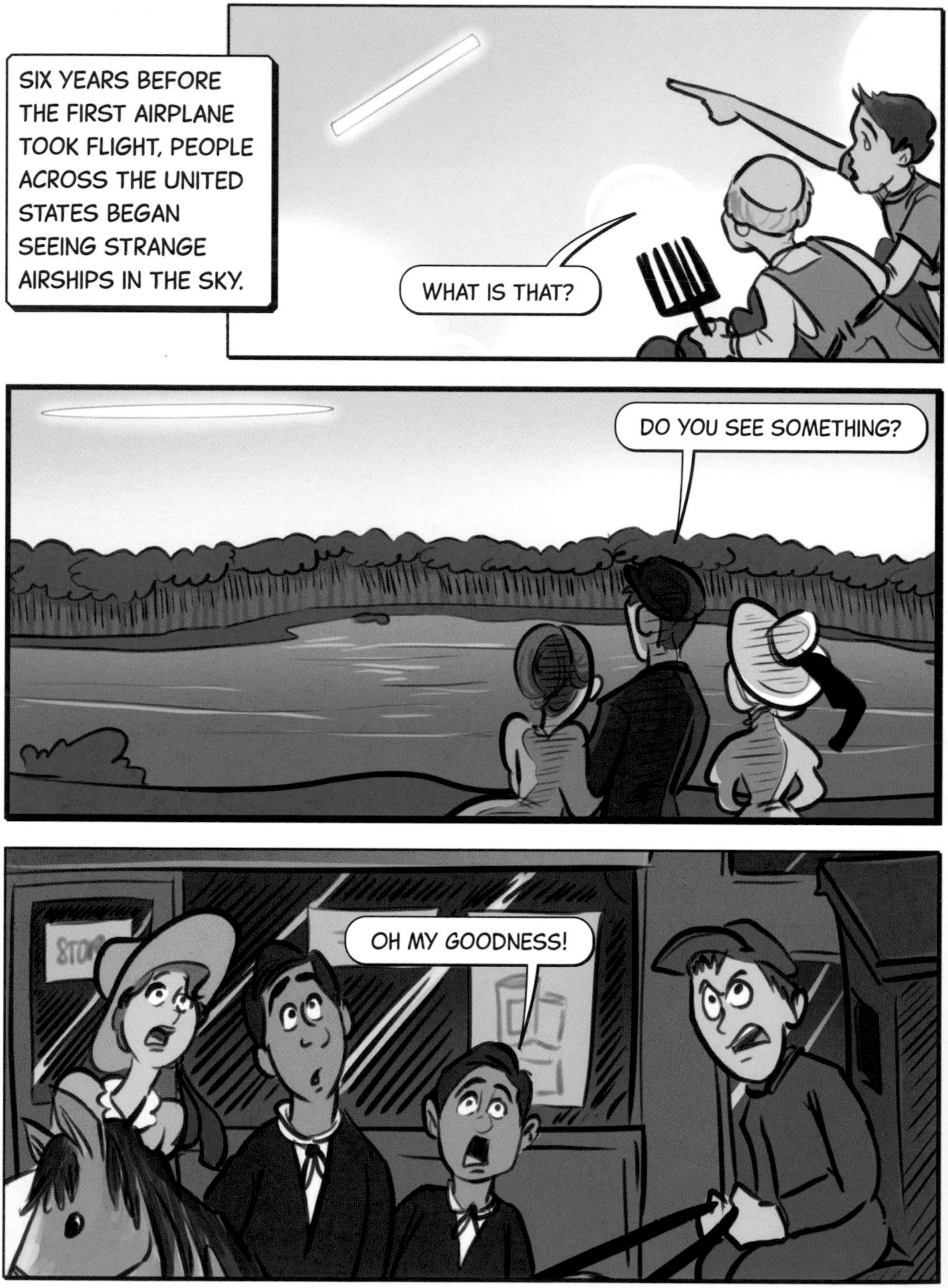

SIX YEARS BEFORE THE FIRST AIRPLANE TOOK FLIGHT, PEOPLE ACROSS THE UNITED STATES BEGAN SEEING STRANGE AIRSHIPS IN THE SKY.
WHAT IS THAT?
DO YOU SEE SOMETHING?
OH MY GOODNESS!

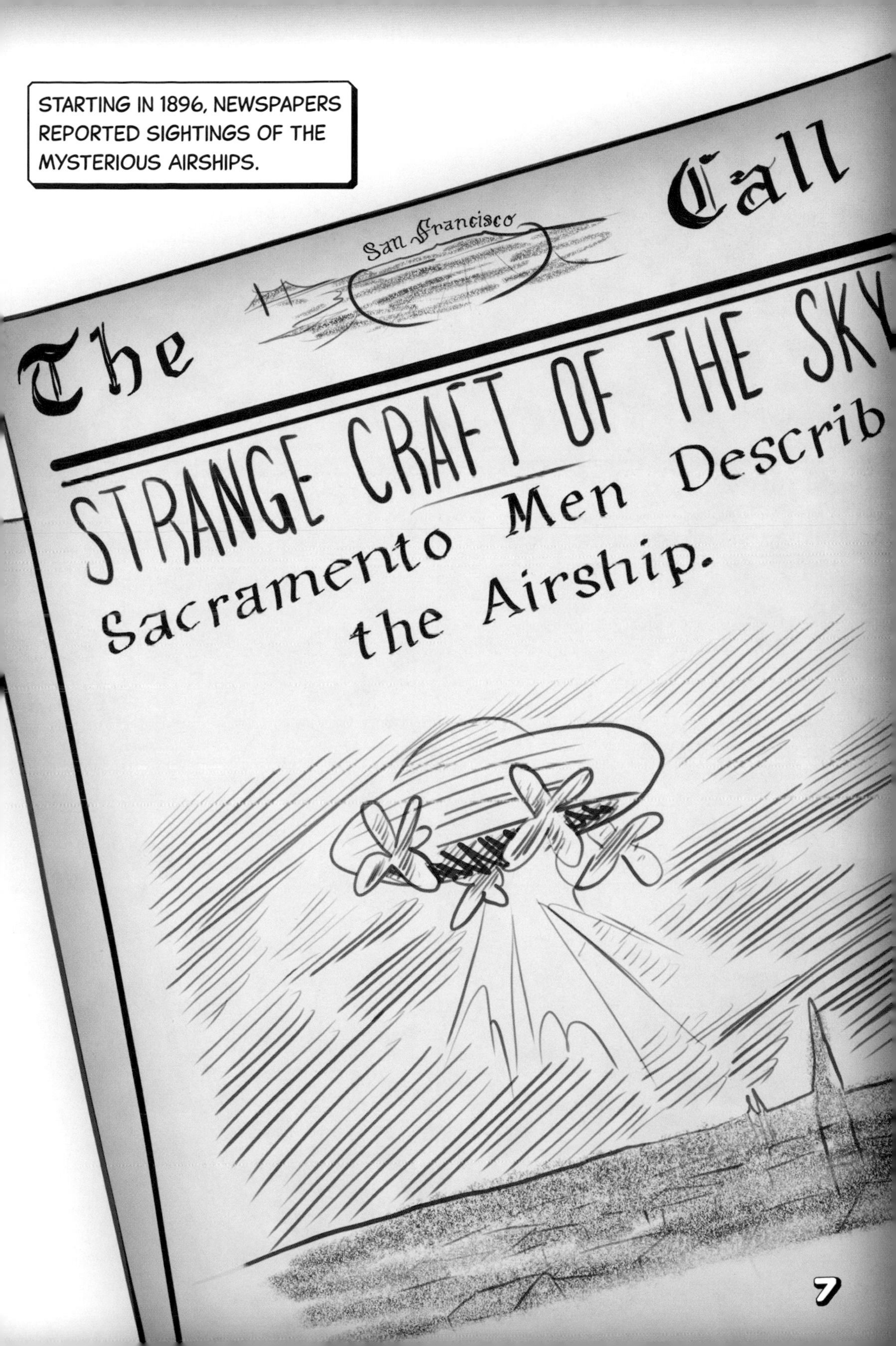
STARTING IN 1896, NEWSPAPERS REPORTED SIGHTINGS OF THE MYSTERIOUS AIRSHIPS.
The San Francisco Call
STRANGE CRAFT OF THE SKY
Sacramento Men Describ
the Airship.

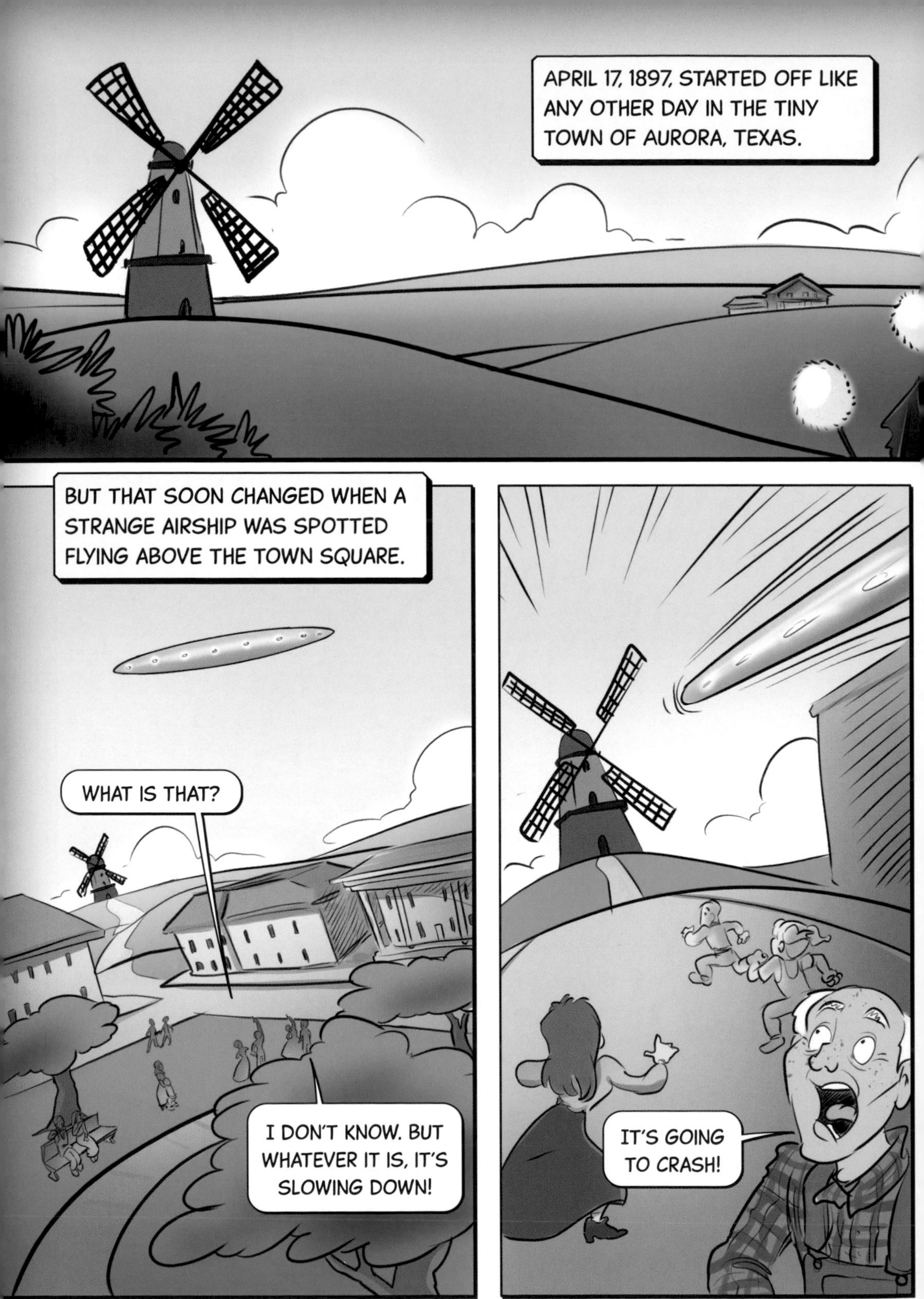
APRIL 17, 1897, STARTED OFF LIKE ANY OTHER DAY IN THE TINY TOWN OF AURORA, TEXAS.
BUT THAT SOON CHANGED WHEN A STRANGE AIRSHIP WAS SPOTTED FLYING ABOVE THE TOWN SQUARE.
WHAT IS THAT?
I DON'T KNOW. BUT WHATEVER IT IS, IT'S SLOWING DOWN!
IT'S GOING TO CRASH!

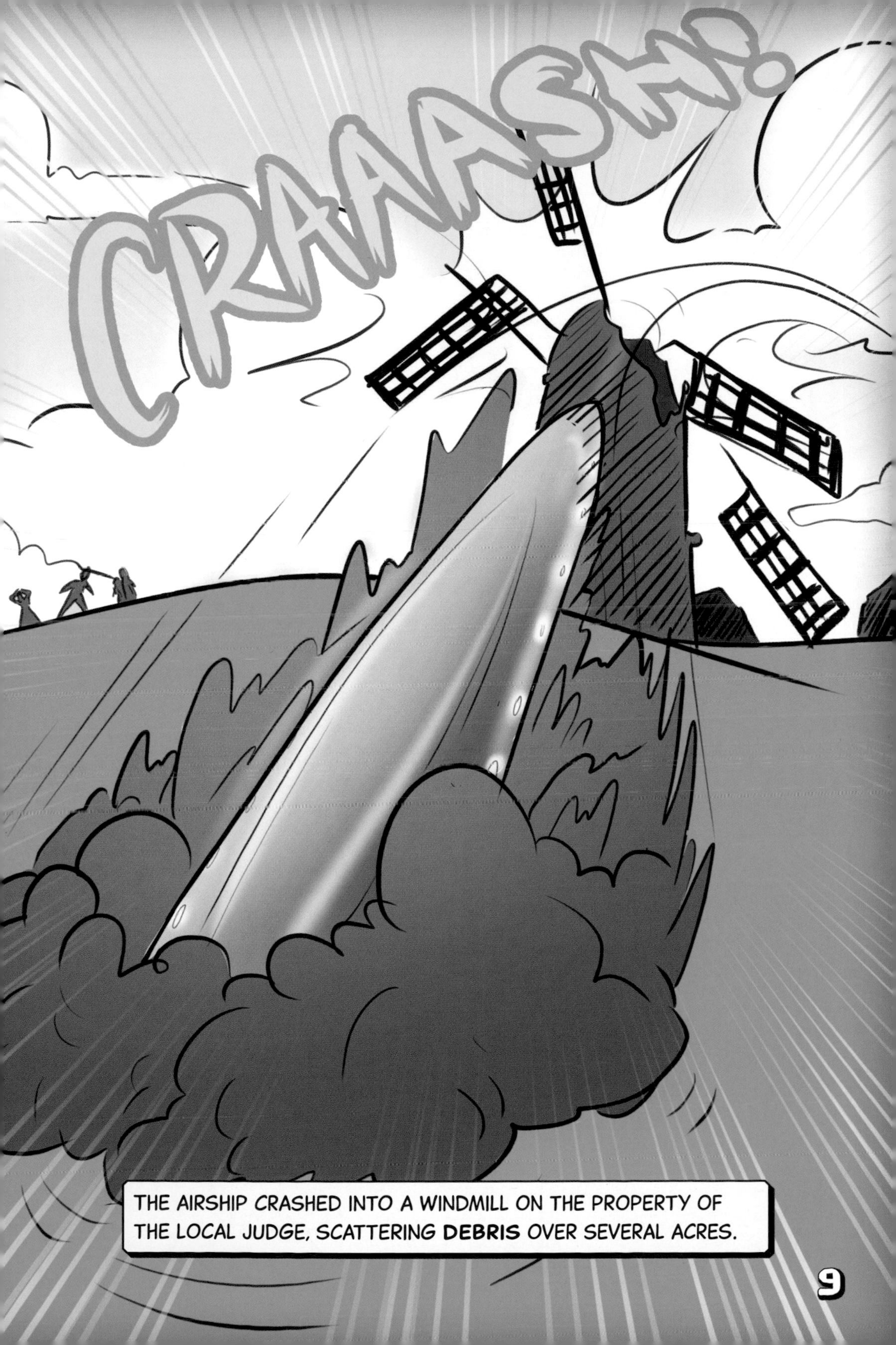
CRAAASH!
THE AIRSHIP CRASHED INTO A WINDMILL ON THE PROPERTY OF THE LOCAL JUDGE, SCATTERING DEBRIS OVER SEVERAL ACRES.

ALIEN FUNERAL

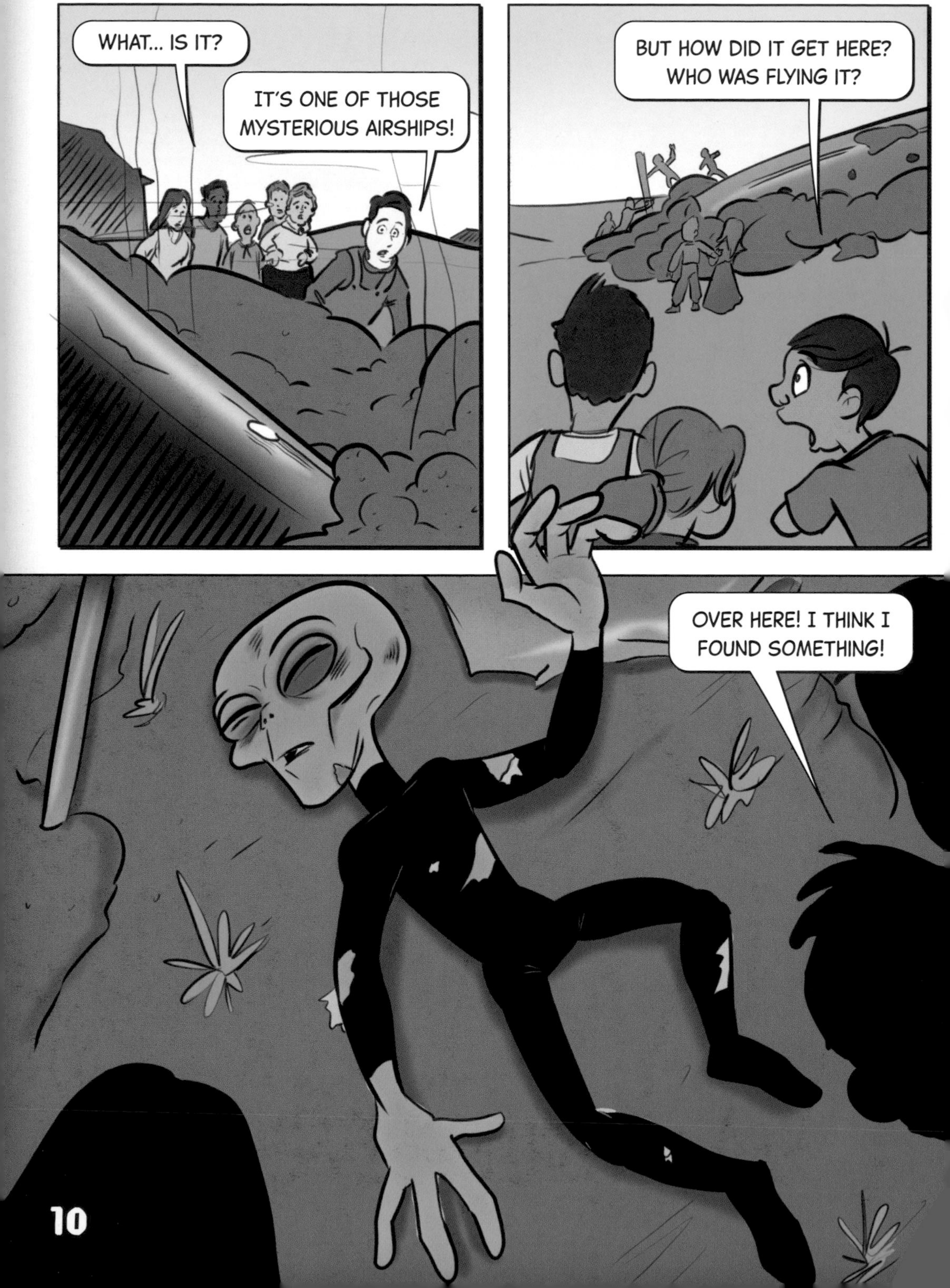

WHAT... IS IT?
IT'S ONE OF THOSE MYSTERIOUS AIRSHIPS!
BUT HOW DID IT GET HERE? WHO WAS FLYING IT?
OVER HERE! I THINK I FOUND SOMETHING!

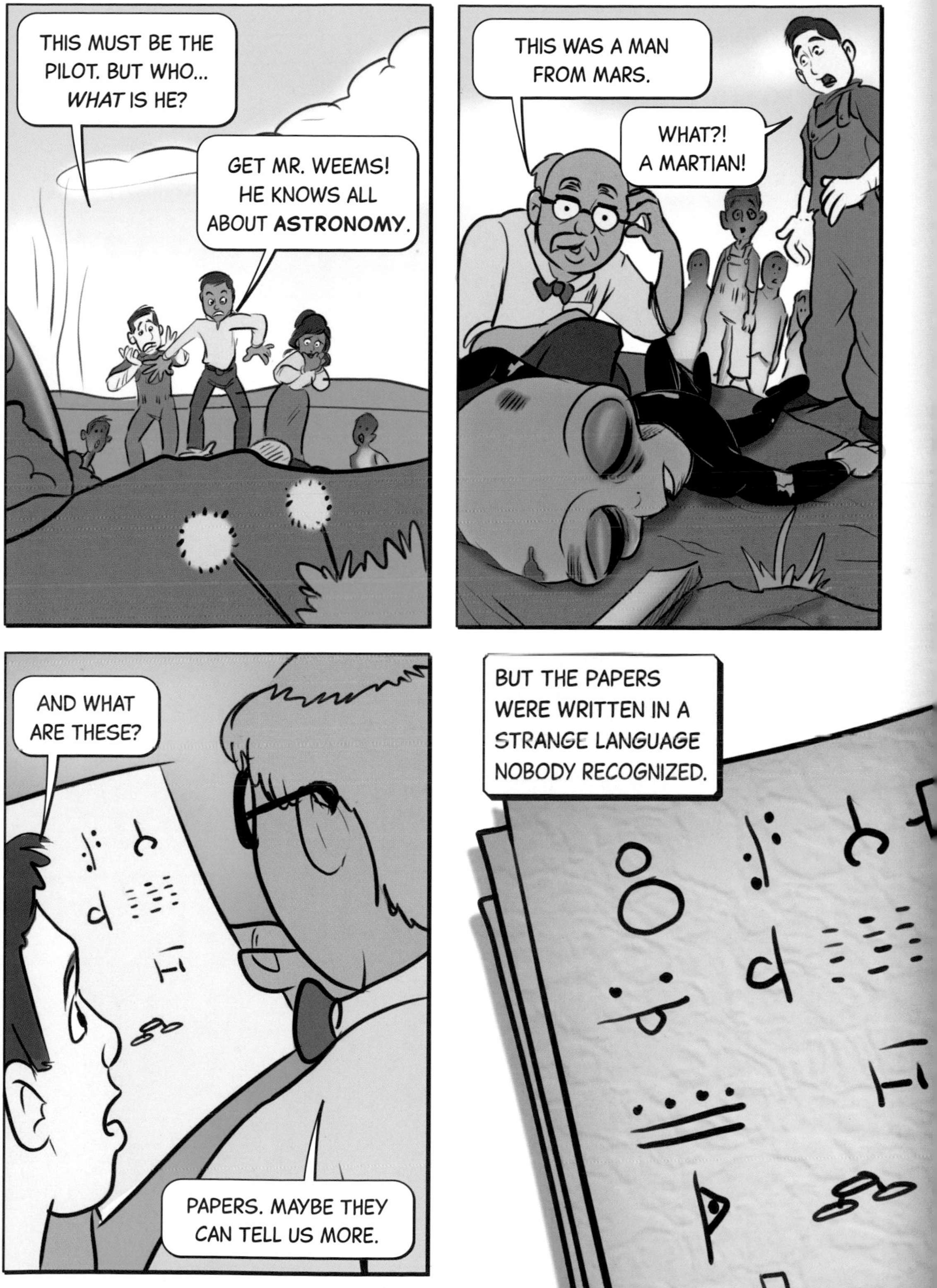
THIS MUST BE THE PILOT. BUT WHO... *WHAT* IS HE?
GET MR. WEEMS! HE KNOWS ALL ABOUT **ASTRONOMY**.
THIS WAS A MAN FROM MARS.
WHAT?! A MARTIAN!
AND WHAT ARE THESE?
PAPERS. MAYBE THEY CAN TELL US MORE.
BUT THE PAPERS WERE WRITTEN IN A STRANGE LANGUAGE NOBODY RECOGNIZED.

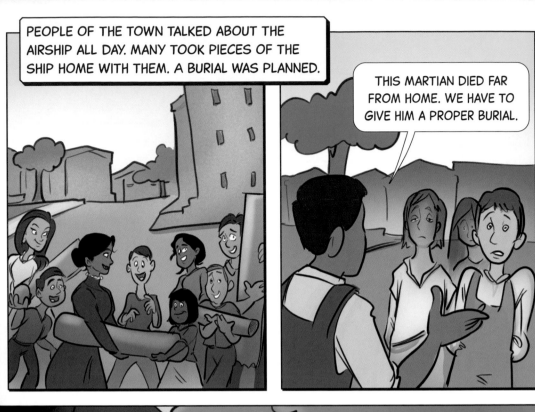

PEOPLE OF THE TOWN TALKED ABOUT THE AIRSHIP ALL DAY. MANY TOOK PIECES OF THE SHIP HOME WITH THEM. A BURIAL WAS PLANNED.

THIS MARTIAN DIED FAR FROM HOME. WE HAVE TO GIVE HIM A PROPER BURIAL.

THE NEXT DAY, SOME PEOPLE FROM THE TOWN GATHERED AT THE CEMETERY.

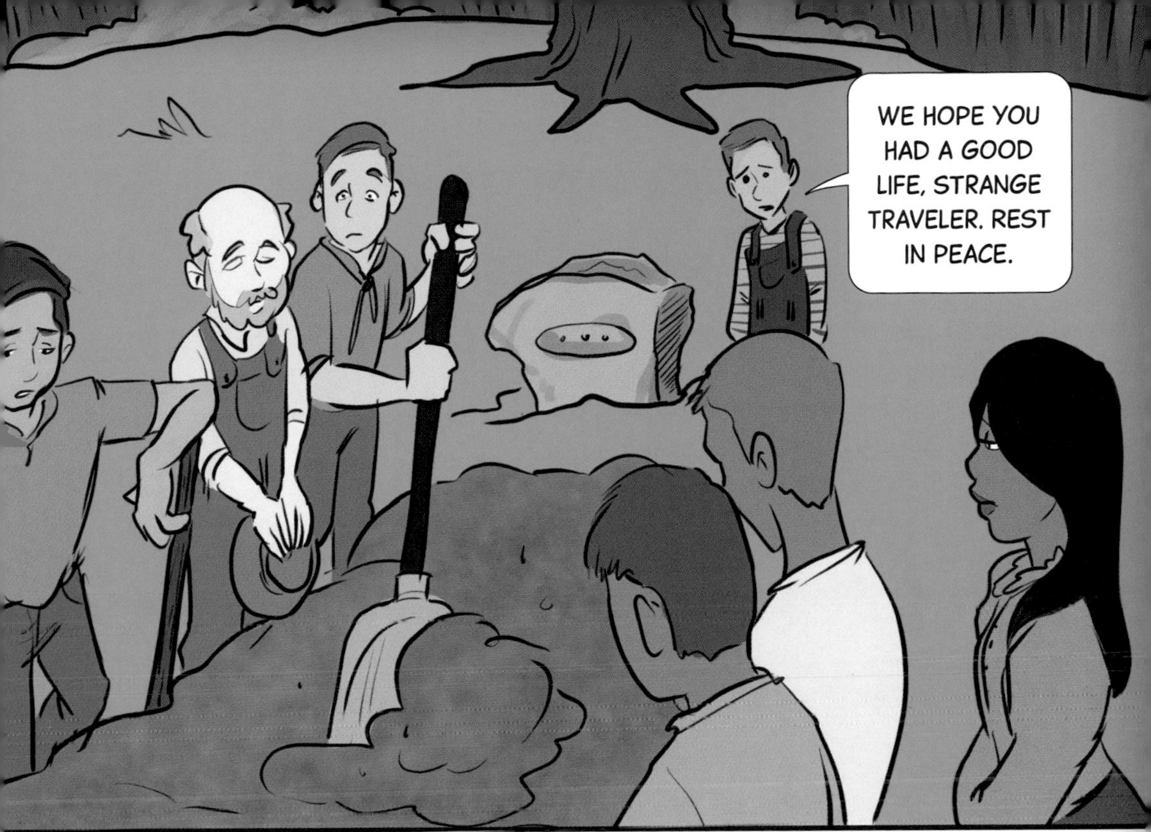
WE HOPE YOU HAD A GOOD LIFE, STRANGE TRAVELER. REST IN PEACE.

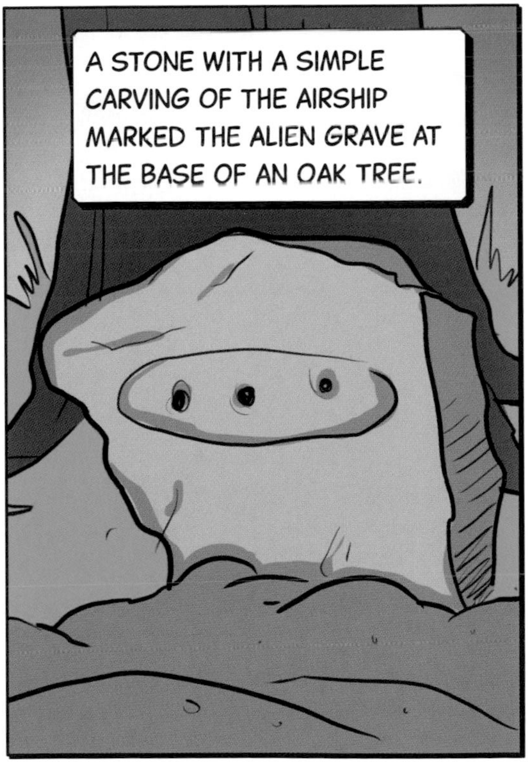
A STONE WITH A SIMPLE CARVING OF THE AIRSHIP MARKED THE ALIEN GRAVE AT THE BASE OF AN OAK TREE.

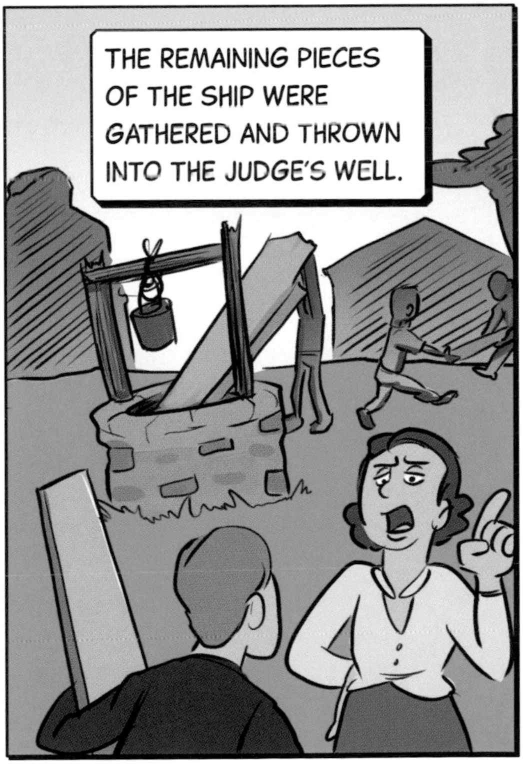
THE REMAINING PIECES OF THE SHIP WERE GATHERED AND THROWN INTO THE JUDGE'S WELL.

TESTING THE WRECK

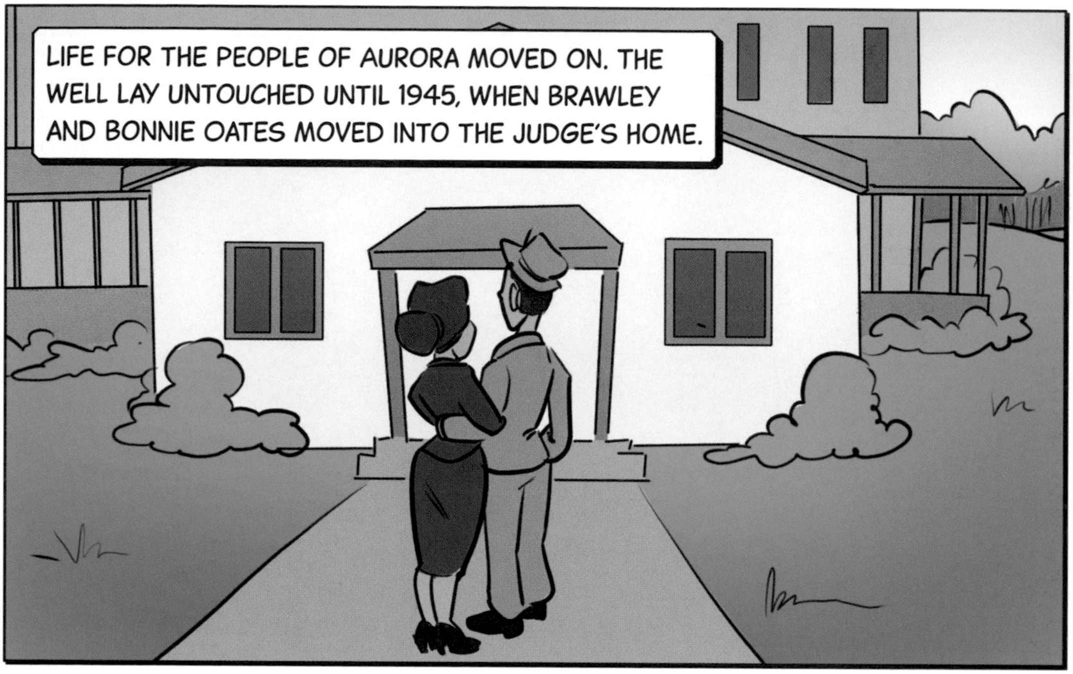
LIFE FOR THE PEOPLE OF AURORA MOVED ON. THE WELL LAY UNTOUCHED UNTIL 1945, WHEN BRAWLEY AND BONNIE OATES MOVED INTO THE JUDGE'S HOME.

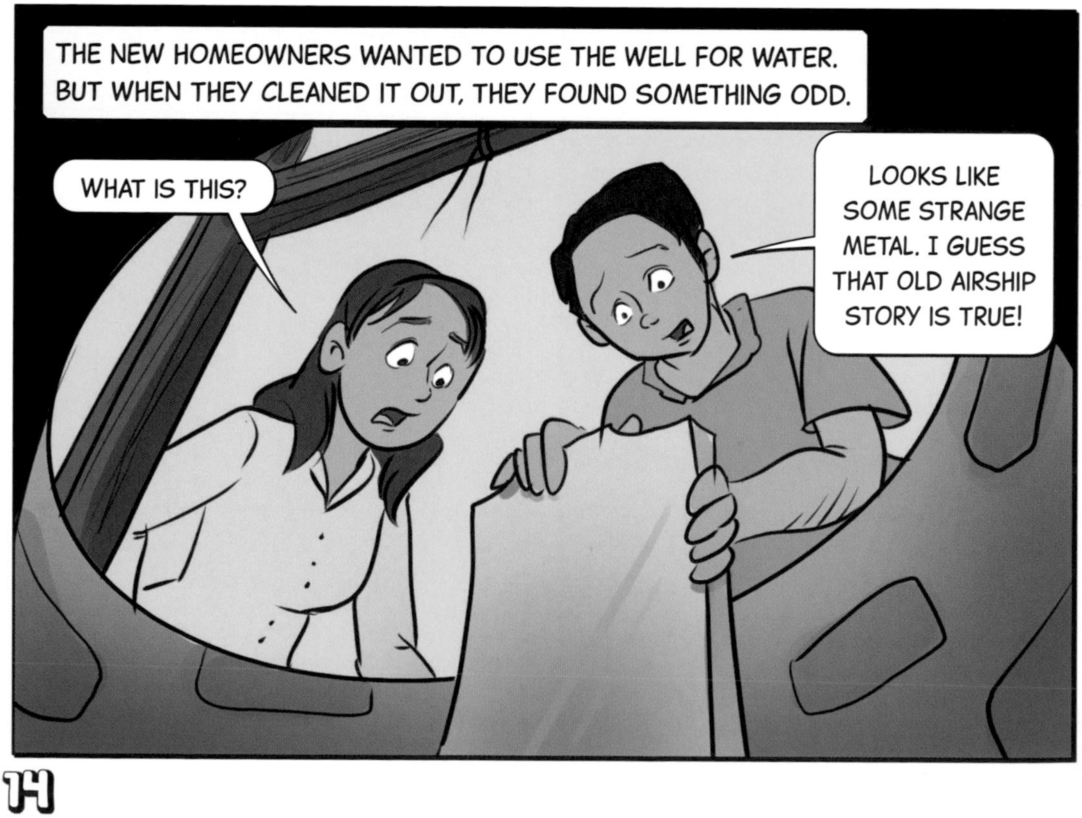
THE NEW HOMEOWNERS WANTED TO USE THE WELL FOR WATER. BUT WHEN THEY CLEANED IT OUT, THEY FOUND SOMETHING ODD.
WHAT IS THIS?
LOOKS LIKE SOME STRANGE METAL. I GUESS THAT OLD AIRSHIP STORY IS TRUE!

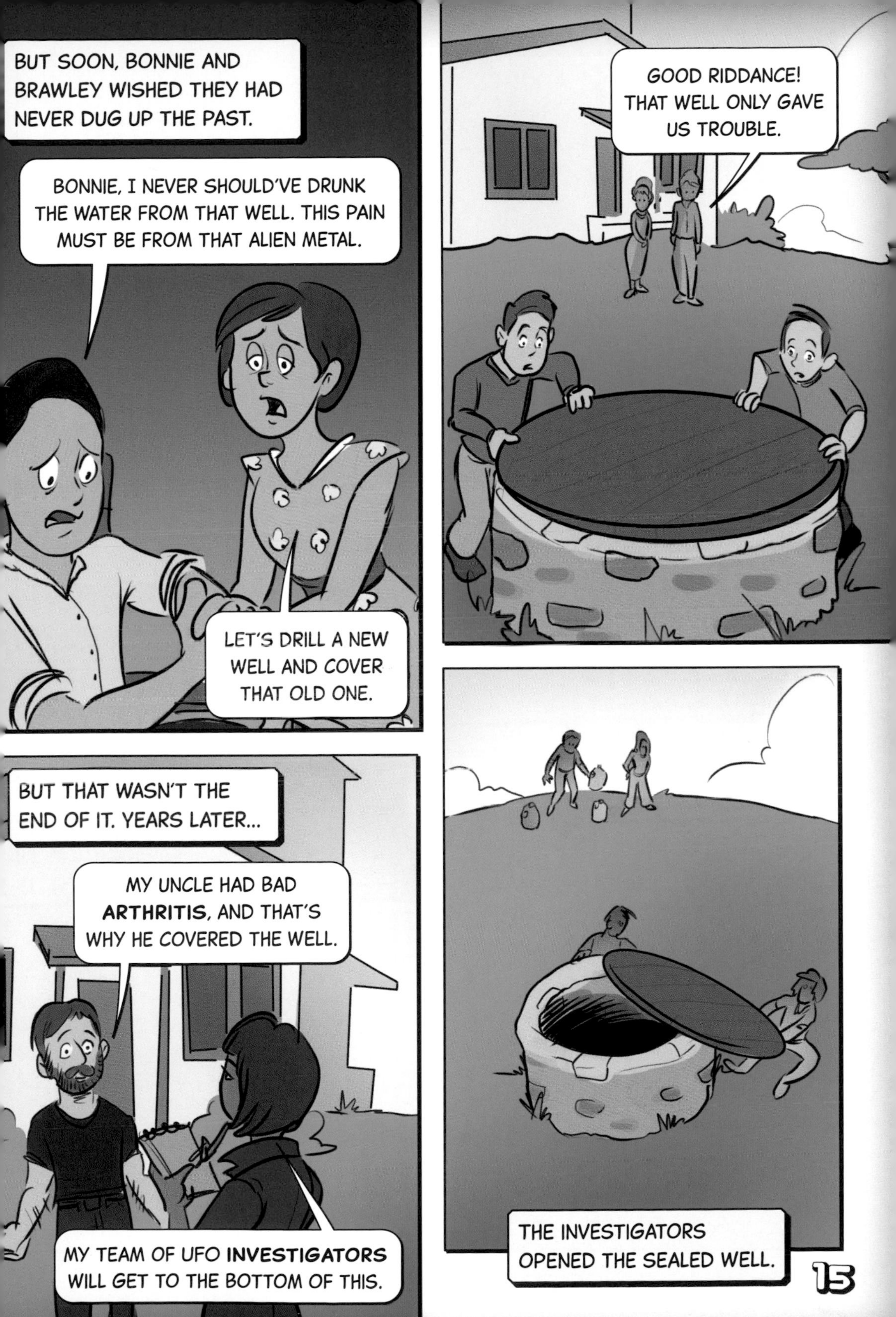

BUT SOON, BONNIE AND BRAWLEY WISHED THEY HAD NEVER DUG UP THE PAST.
BONNIE, I NEVER SHOULD'VE DRUNK THE WATER FROM THAT WELL. THIS PAIN MUST BE FROM THAT ALIEN METAL.
LET'S DRILL A NEW WELL AND COVER THAT OLD ONE.
GOOD RIDDANCE! THAT WELL ONLY GAVE US TROUBLE.
BUT THAT WASN'T THE END OF IT. YEARS LATER...
MY UNCLE HAD BAD **ARTHRITIS**, AND THAT'S WHY HE COVERED THE WELL.
MY TEAM OF UFO **INVESTIGATORS** WILL GET TO THE BOTTOM OF THIS.
THE INVESTIGATORS OPENED THE SEALED WELL.

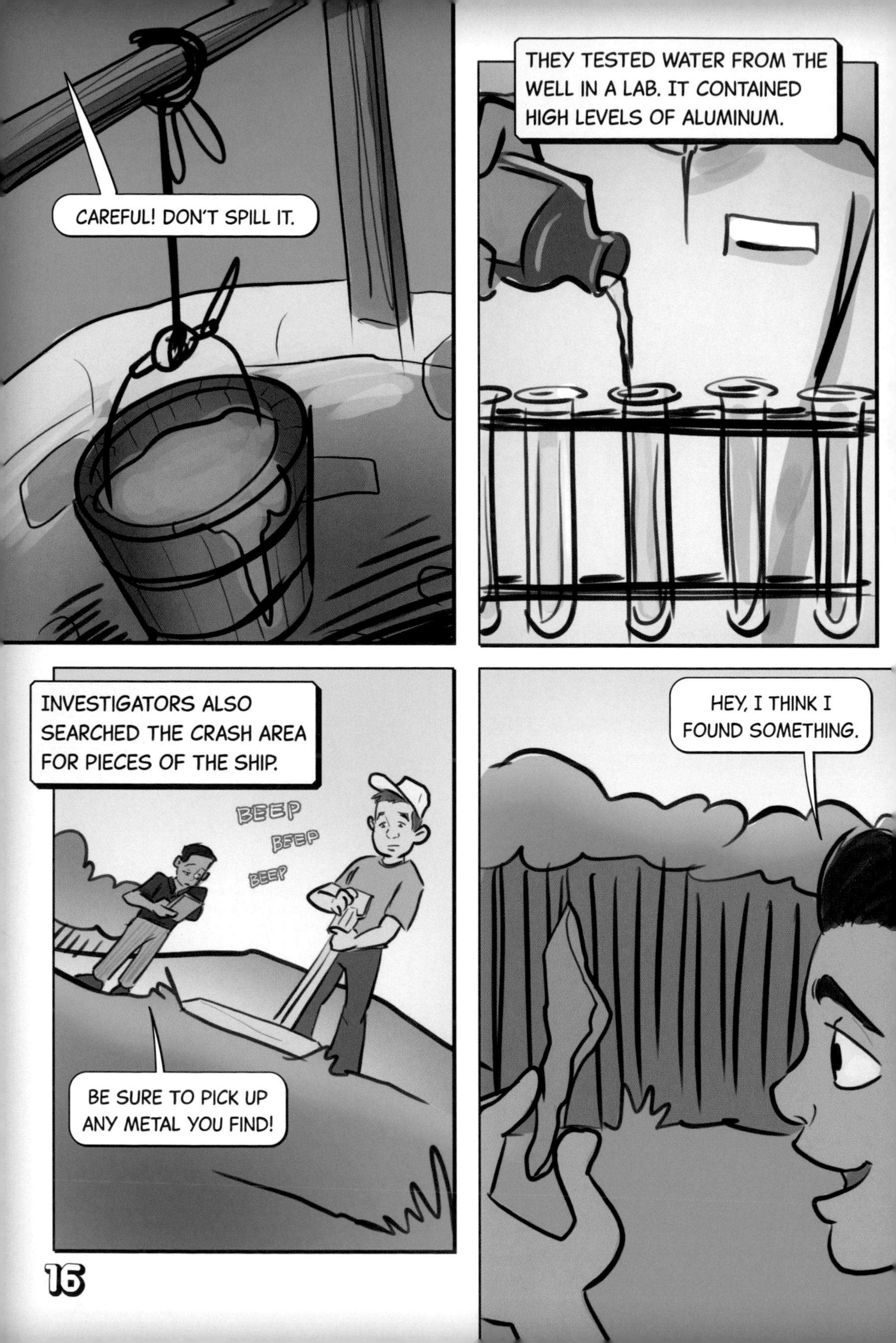
CAREFUL! DON'T SPILL IT.
THEY TESTED WATER FROM THE WELL IN A LAB. IT CONTAINED HIGH LEVELS OF ALUMINUM.
INVESTIGATORS ALSO SEARCHED THE CRASH AREA FOR PIECES OF THE SHIP.
BEEP
BEEP
BEEP
BE SURE TO PICK UP ANY METAL YOU FIND!
HEY, I THINK I FOUND SOMETHING.

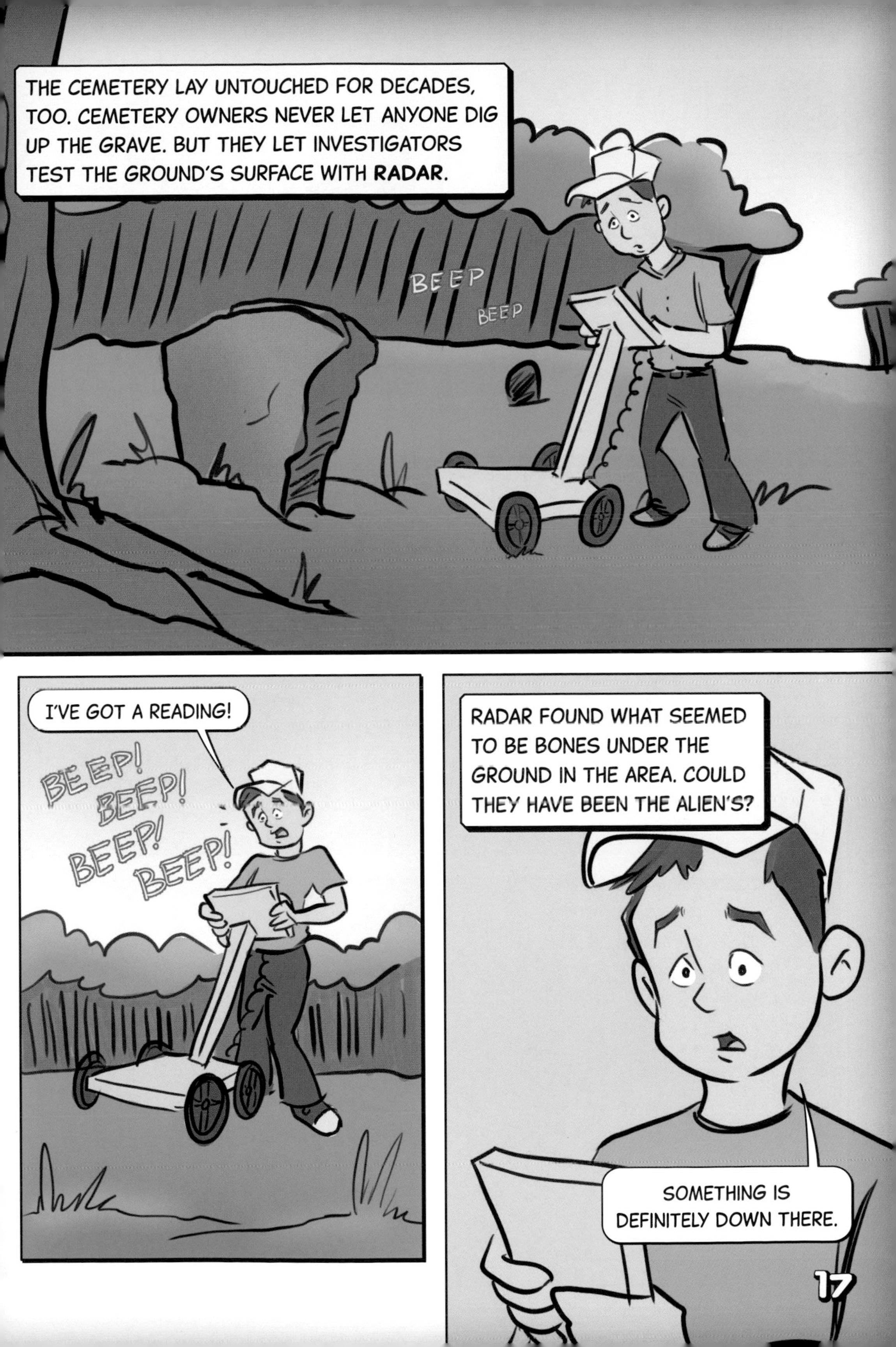
THE CEMETERY LAY UNTOUCHED FOR DECADES, TOO. CEMETERY OWNERS NEVER LET ANYONE DIG UP THE GRAVE. BUT THEY LET INVESTIGATORS TEST THE GROUND'S SURFACE WITH **RADAR**.
BEEP
BEEP
I'VE GOT A READING!
BEEP!
BEEP!
BEEP!
BEEP!
RADAR FOUND WHAT SEEMED TO BE BONES UNDER THE GROUND IN THE AREA. COULD THEY HAVE BEEN THE ALIEN'S?
SOMETHING IS DEFINITELY DOWN THERE.

A HOAX?

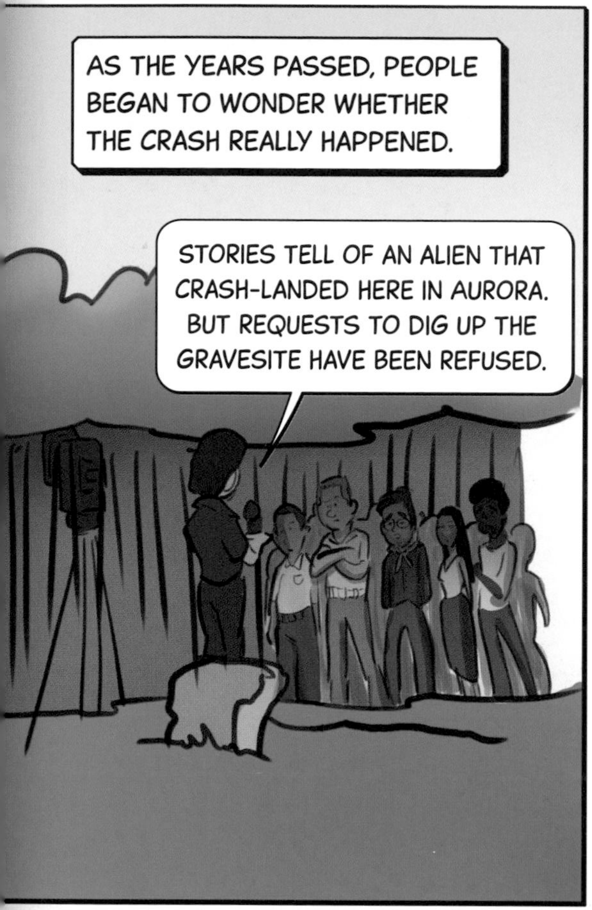
AS THE YEARS PASSED, PEOPLE BEGAN TO WONDER WHETHER THE CRASH REALLY HAPPENED.
STORIES TELL OF AN ALIEN THAT CRASH-LANDED HERE IN AURORA. BUT REQUESTS TO DIG UP THE GRAVESITE HAVE BEEN REFUSED.

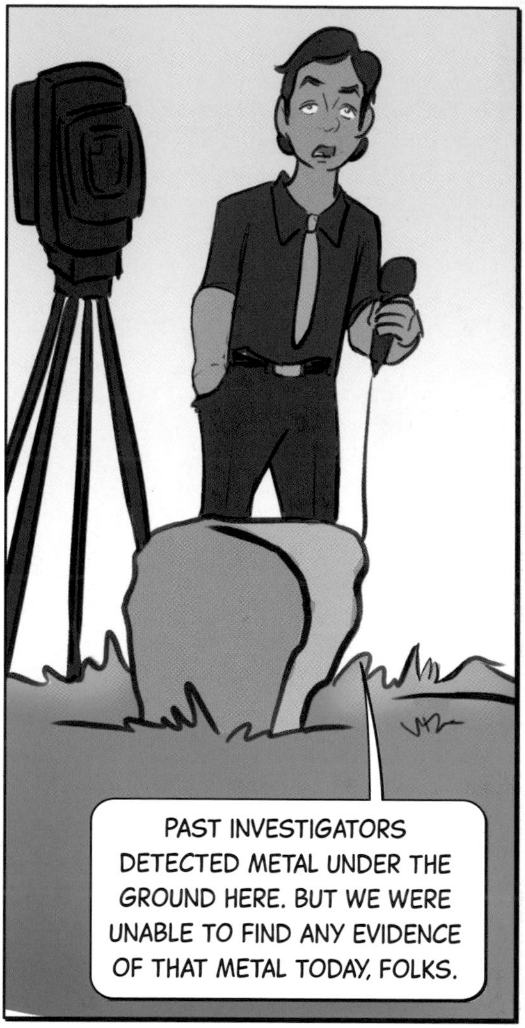
PAST INVESTIGATORS DETECTED METAL UNDER THE GROUND HERE. BUT WE WERE UNABLE TO FIND ANY EVIDENCE OF THAT METAL TODAY, FOLKS.

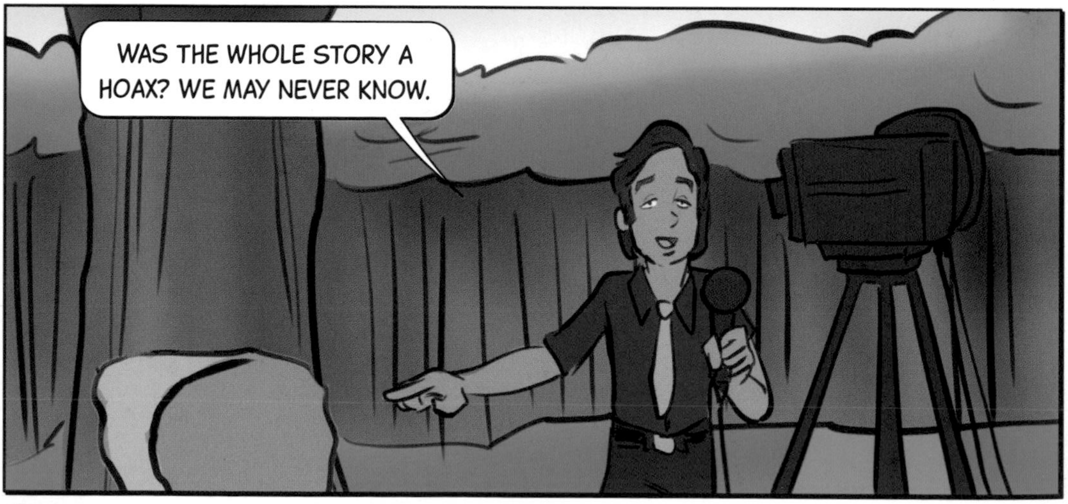
WAS THE WHOLE STORY A HOAX? WE MAY NEVER KNOW.

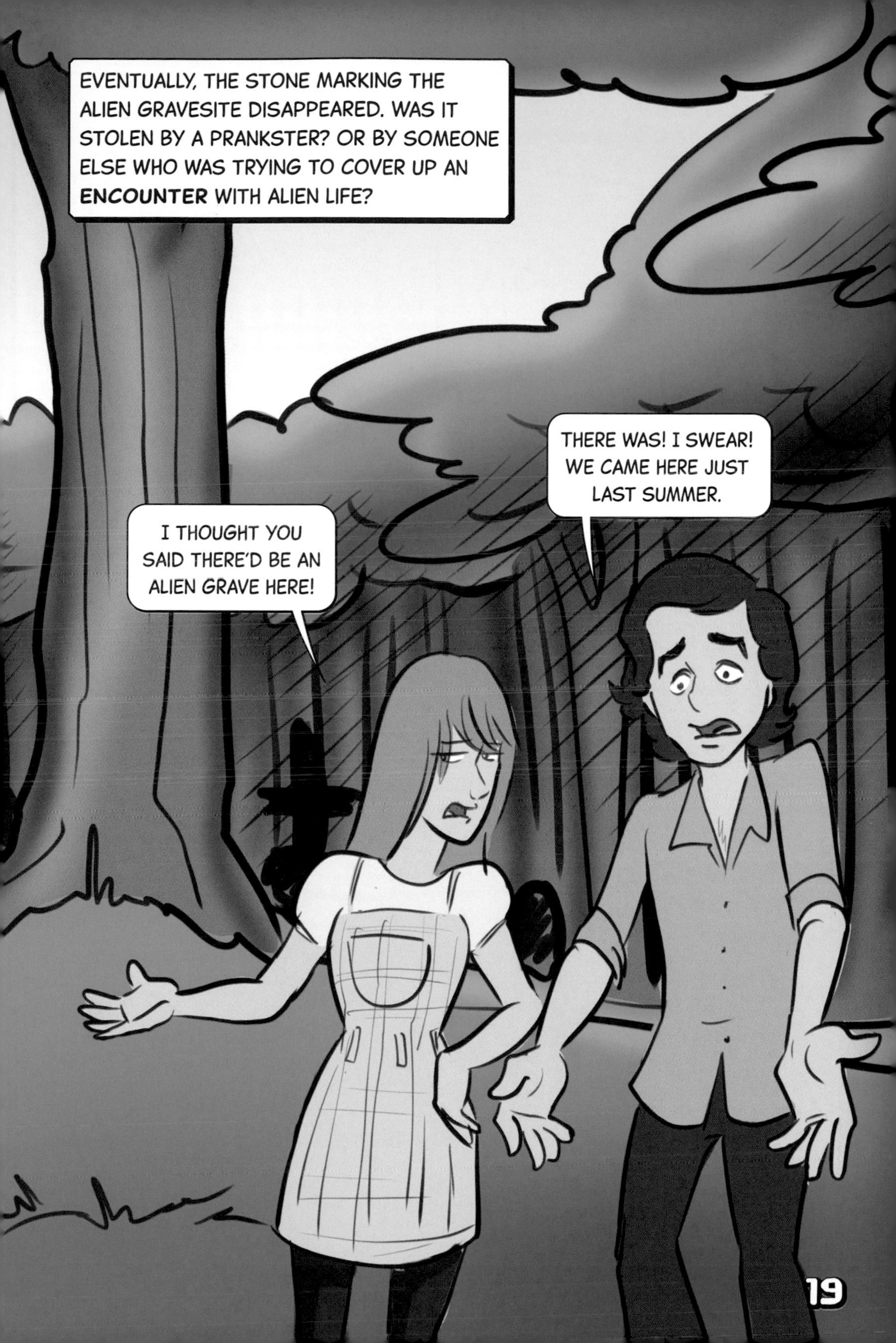

EVENTUALLY, THE STONE MARKING THE ALIEN GRAVESITE DISAPPEARED. WAS IT STOLEN BY A PRANKSTER? OR BY SOMEONE ELSE WHO WAS TRYING TO COVER UP AN **ENCOUNTER** WITH ALIEN LIFE?
I THOUGHT YOU SAID THERE'D BE AN ALIEN GRAVE HERE!
THERE WAS! I SWEAR! WE CAME HERE JUST LAST SUMMER.

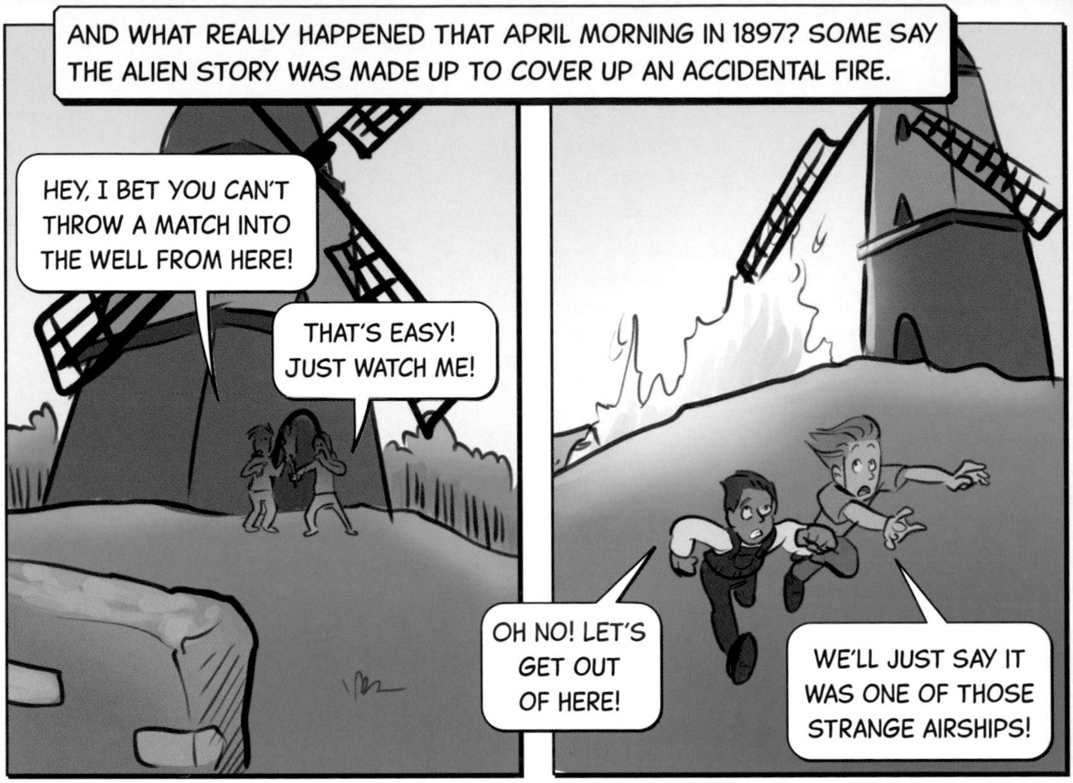
AND WHAT REALLY HAPPENED THAT APRIL MORNING IN 1897? SOME SAY THE ALIEN STORY WAS MADE UP TO COVER UP AN ACCIDENTAL FIRE.
HEY, I BET YOU CAN'T THROW A MATCH INTO THE WELL FROM HERE!
THAT'S EASY! JUST WATCH ME!
OH NO! LET'S GET OUT OF HERE!
WE'LL JUST SAY IT WAS ONE OF THOSE STRANGE AIRSHIPS!

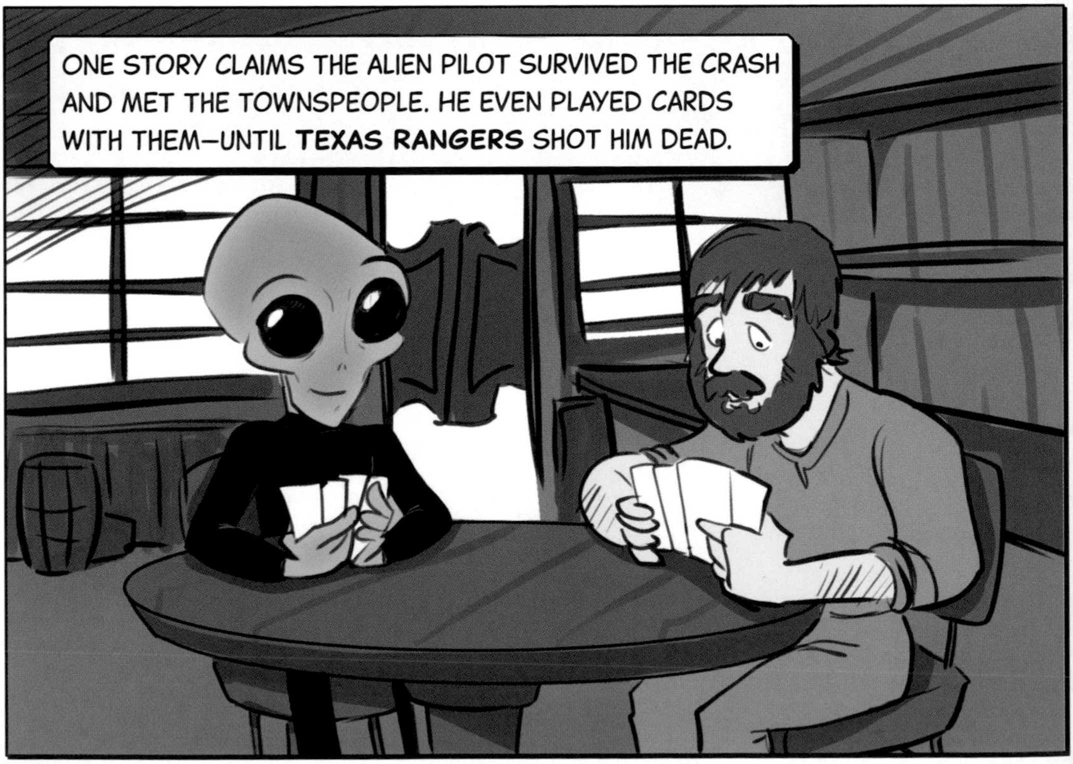
ONE STORY CLAIMS THE ALIEN PILOT SURVIVED THE CRASH AND MET THE TOWNSPEOPLE. HE EVEN PLAYED CARDS WITH THEM—UNTIL **TEXAS RANGERS** SHOT HIM DEAD.

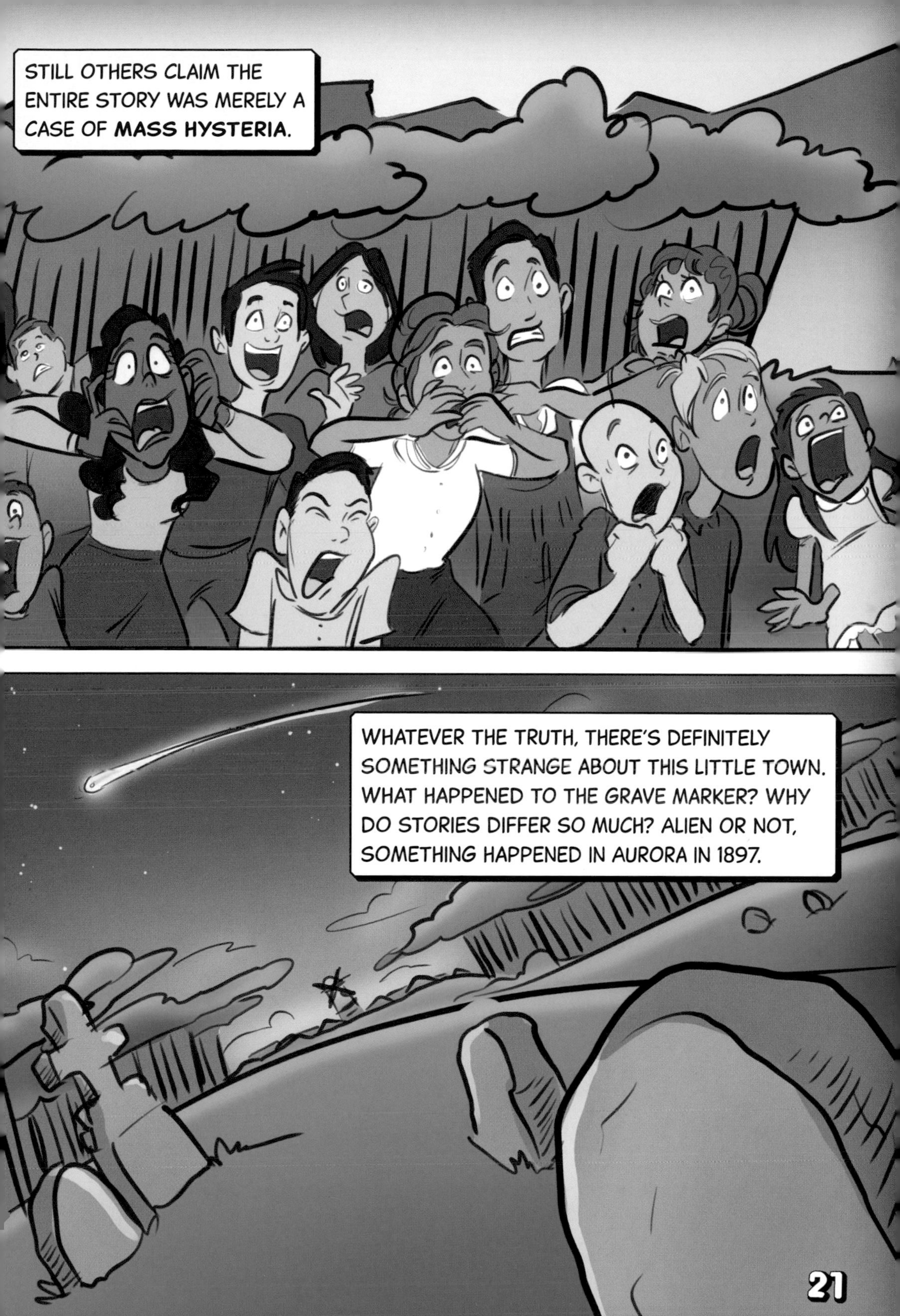
STILL OTHERS CLAIM THE ENTIRE STORY WAS MERELY A CASE OF **MASS HYSTERIA**.
WHATEVER THE TRUTH, THERE'S DEFINITELY SOMETHING STRANGE ABOUT THIS LITTLE TOWN. WHAT HAPPENED TO THE GRAVE MARKER? WHY DO STORIES DIFFER SO MUCH? ALIEN OR NOT, SOMETHING HAPPENED IN AURORA IN 1897.

OTHER TERRIFYING ALIEN ENCOUNTERS

ROSWELL

ROSWELL, NEW MEXICO

UFO CRASH SITE
UFO Museum - 114 N. Main - Roswell

On June 13, 1947, a New Mexico rancher named Mac Brazel heard a loud explosion. The next day, he found pieces of metal and a long trench in the ground. It was as if a large object had crashed. The local sheriff contacted the army base nearby. On July 8, an army officer said the metal may have been from an alien spaceship. The next day, however, the army said the wreckage was just a weather balloon. Was the army hiding the truth?

RENDLESHAM FOREST

SUFFOLK, ENGLAND

At 3:00 a.m. on December 26, 1980, members of the U.S. Air Force saw bright lights flashing in the night sky. The servicemen then saw a glowing object hovering in the air above Rendlesham Forest. Sergeant Jim Penniston got close enough to touch the warm metal on the outside of a UFO before it took off into the sky. In the morning, the servicemen returned to the site. They saw three small holes in the ground. The branches of nearby trees were broken and burned. No one can agree on—or explain—exactly what or who left behind the mysterious marks.

GLOSSARY

arthritis a painful disease that makes the joints in a body swollen and stiff

astronomy the study of outer space

debris the pieces of buildings or other objects that have been destroyed or damaged

encounter an unexpected meeting, often unpleasant

evidence objects or information that can be used to prove whether something is true

investigators people who try to find out as much as possible about something

mass hysteria a condition in which a group of people feels fear or panic that keeps them from thinking clearly

radar a tool that can find the location of an object by sending out radio waves, which hit the object and bounce back to form an image on a computer screen

Texas Rangers a group of armed men, like a police force, in Texas

universe everything that exists on Earth and in the rest of space

INDEX

READ MORE

Morey, Allan. *Alien Invasion (It's the End of the World!).* Minneapolis: Bellwether Media, Inc. (2020).

Murray, Laura K. *Aliens (Are They Real?).* Mankato, MN: Creative Education (2017).

Williams, Dinah. *UFO Crash Sites (Scary Places).* New York: Bearport Publishing (2015).

LEARN MORE ONLINE

1. Go to **www.factsurfer.com**

2. Enter "**Alien Graveyard**" into the search box.

3. Click on the cover of this book to see a list of websites.